The last ETHNIC CLEANSING in EUROPE
and the response of the INTERNATIONAL COMMUNITY

By :

ALEKSANDAR KITANOVSKI PhD
Skopje,Macedonia

CONTENTS :

Abstract

In this research paper I will look at the 'ethnic cleansing' of the Muslims by the Serbs in Bosnia-Herzegovina between 1992 and late 1995. This is not to say atrocities were not committed by or against any other parties during the war. But as has been clearly proven the majority was committed by Serbs minority against the Muslims and this was in accordance with an overall policy of the Serbs in pursuit of a Greater Serbia. Thereafter, I will look at the response of the 'international community' towards the conflict and tragedy. This paper will show that the international community throughout the conflict accepted aggression.

In this paper I refer to the "Muslims" and not the Bosnians. This I do because the Serb policy was directed especially towards the Muslims and not "Bosnians" in general, and they were the main victims.

In chapter one, I will look at the ethnic cleansing and atrocities committed by the Serbs against the Muslims. I will show that the acts were systematic and in accordance with the overall Serb policy.

In chapter two, I will look at three major players in the international community who were expected to become involved in the crisis, namely US, EC and UN. I will look at the factors which affected their reactions and also the implications of their response.

In chapter three, I will look at three courses of action namely military intervention, air strikes and lifting the arms embargo. Thereafter, I will look at the issue of 'safe areas' and the effects of establishing them during the conflict.

In chapter four, I will look at certain misconceptions regarding the crisis and their implications.

Finally, in chapter five, I will show that the international community accepted and rewarded Serbian aggression and ethnic cleansing.

List of Abbreviations :

CIA - Central Intelligence Agency
EC - European Community
GDR - German Democratic Republic
IFOR - Implementation Force
JNA - Yugoslav People's Army
NATO - North Atlantic Treaty Organisation
OSCE - Organisation for Security and Co-operation in Europe
SDA - Party for Democratic Action
UK - United kingdom
UN - United Nations
UNHCR - United Nations High Commission/Commissioner for   Refugees
UNPROFOR - United Nations Protection Force
US - United States

INTRODUCTION

Bosnia-Herzegovina with Slovenia, Croatia, Macedonia, Serbia and Montenegro made up the former Socialist Federal Republic of Yugoslavia. After the Second World War the people were brought together and controlled by the communist president, Josip Broz Tito. After Tito's death (1980) the country began to disintegrate. Various reasons can be mentioned as to the cause, including economic decline, but a major cause was nationalism, Slobodan Milosevic and his aspirations of a Greater Serbia.

Since the mid 80s /90s Serbian intellectuals and even the church had started to develop a nationalist agenda. In 1986-87 the Serbian Academy of Arts and Sciences structured a Serbian memorandum, stating that the goal of a Greater Serbia uniting all Serbs regardless of their original republic still existed.1 Milosevic used the sentiment of nationalism to rise to power. He took control of the media and launched a campaign against everything non-Serb. Serbs were made to believe that they had been victimised for centuries, and even at the time were being discriminated against and victimised by non-Serbs.2 However, Muslims in Bosnia were a major obstacle in the path of Milosevic and the Serbian nationalists. For due to their large numbers they could determine whether or not Bosnia would become part of a Greater Serbia. Muslims were portrayed as the 'other' and isolated for discrimination and victimisation, by the intellectuals, orientalists, the clergy and the government. Thus, the preparation for the ethnic cleansing of the Muslims had begun.3

In January 1992, Germany recognised Slovenia and Croatia as independent states.4 This was after the Yugoslav People's Army and Serbia had launched an attack on both and taken control of a third of Croatia. Fearing Serb domination, in December 1991, the Bosnian Parliament also voted and asked for independence. They were told to hold a referendum, which took place on the end of February 1992. 63% of the total population turned out and 99% voted in favour of independence.5 On 7 April 1992, the European Community (EC) and the United States (US) recognised Bosnia-Herzegovina as an independent state.6 However, fighting had already started from the week beginning 22 March and by April 1992, two thirds of Bosnia-Herzegovina was in Serb control.7   The war brought with it atrocities, mass expulsions, mass graves, concentration camps, systematic rape, ethnic cleansing and genocide.

References for Introduction

1. Norman Cigar, Genocide in Bosnia. The Policy of Ethnic Cleansing, College Station: Texas A & M University Press, 1995, p. 24

2. Christopher Bennett, Yugoslavia's Bloody Collapse. Causes, Course and Consequences, London: Hurst & Company, 1995, pp. 96-98

3. Cigar, op. cit.

4. Misha Glenny, The fall of Yugoslavia, The Third Balkan War, London: Penguin Books, 1993, p. 163

5. Bennett, op. cit., p. 186

6. Glenny, op. cit., p. 167

7. Mark Thompson, 'The Final Solution of Bosnia-Herzegovina' 1992, In Rabia Ali and Lawrence Lifschultz (eds), Why Bosnia? Writings of the Balkan War, Stony Creek: The Pamphleteer's Press, Inc., 1993, p. 175

CHAPTER ONE
ETHNIC CLEANSING

As Andrew Bell-Fialkoff has pointed out cleansing is not a phenomenon that falls easily into definable terms. It covers a wide range of practices including deportation, expulsion, mass population transfers, light pressure to emigrate and its most extreme form is genocide. It is not a practice carried out solely upon ethnic groups but can also be applied to groups characterised by religion, class and race among others. Bell-Fialkoff has defined population cleansing as "a planned, deliberate, removal from a certain territory of an undesirable population distinguished by one or more characteristics such as ethnicity, religion, race, class or sexual preference."[1]

The term ethnic cleansing was introduced by the Serbs[2] and has passed into the English language from the Serbo-Croat term 'etnicko ciscenje'.[3] Similar terms were also used by the Nazis in their campaign against the Jews, for example 'selbsttreingung' (self-cleansing) and 'Judensauberung' (the cleansing of the Jews).[4]

According to Theodor Meron:
ethnic cleansing consists of harassment, discrimination, beatings, torture, summary executions, expulsions, forced crossing of the lines between combatants, intimidation, destruction of secular and religious property, mass and systematic rape, arbitrary arrests and executions, deliberate military attacks on civilians and civilian property, uses of siege and cutting of essential supplies destined for civilian populations. Many of these methods, considered in isolation, constitute a war crime or a grave breach. Considered as a cluster of violations, these practices also constitute crimes against humanity and perhaps also crimes under the Genocide Convention. [5]

The United Nations terms as:
crimes against humanity. . . . the following crimes when committed in armed conflict, whether international or internal in character, and directed against any civilian population:
(a) murder;
(b) exterminations;
(c) enslavement;
(d) deportation;
(e) imprisonment;
(f) torture;
(g) rape;
(h) persecutions on political, racial and religious grounds;
(i) other inhumane acts.[6]

Article two of the United Nations Convention on the Prevention and Punishment of the crime of Genocide states:

Genocide means any of the following acts committed with intent to destroy, in whole or in part, a national, ethnical, racial or religious group, as such:

(a) Killing members of the group;
(b) Causing bodily or mental harm to members of the group;
(c) Deliberately inflicting on the group conditions of life calculated to bring about its physical destruction in whole or in part;
(d) Imposing measures intended to prevent births within a group;
(e) Forcibly transferring children of the group to another group.[7]

During the war in Bosnia-Herzegovina the exact number of Muslims killed and displaced is practically impossible to ascertain. But, by February 1993 between 250,000 and 270,000 people, 10% of the Muslim population is thought to have died,[8] and by early 1994 almost 2 million people were displaced.[9]

The ethnic cleansing of the Muslims by the Serbs was not ad hoc but was systematic and part of a grand Serbian policy. According to a report in the New York Times, the CIA has concluded that 95% of the acts of ethnic cleansing were carried out by Serbs.[10] Similarly, Philip Cohen in 'Serbia at War with history' has written that by June 1993 the US Department of State submitted to the United Nations eight reports on atrocities and war crimes in former Yugoslavia; 88% were by Serbs, 7% by Bosnian Muslims and 5% by Croats. But 100% of genocidal acts have been committed by Serbs in accordance with Serbian policy.[11]

These are but a few figures, but the nature of the ethnic cleansing of the Muslims by the Serbs, and the manner and ferocity with which it was carried out, cannot easily be described by words. It was such that according to David Rieff it does not justify being called a war but has to be called a slaughter.[12] And Haris Silajdzic, initially the Foreign Minister and then the Prime Minister of Bosnia said, "what is going on is genocide. In the West, many people choose to call it war. But it's not war; it's slaughter."[13] A few examples are given here to show the plight of the victims.

As the ethnic cleansing got under way, during May 1992 between 180 and 200 houses shops and mosques were being burnt each day and people were putting out pillow cases, sheets etc. as white flags of surrender from windows. This humility also befell a minaret of a mosque near Prijedor. The situation was explained in 'Epoka', a weekly from Belgrade, "If the Muslims do not fly the white flags from the minarets we will flatten those villages, Serbian villages will replace them."[14] Wherever, the Serbian forces went, men of fighting age, usually taken to be fifteen, irrespective of whether they were fighters or just civilians were killed or sent to concentration camps and the women and children were forced to flee or were deported away. Thousands of women, children and old people were transported away from northern Bosnia in sealed freight cars. Hundreds of people were packed into each car for days in which many died. In one such incident the deportees were kept without food or water in the train for four days and were then ordered out of the train in the middle of the night, and told to walk the remaining fifteen miles to the nearest town Maglaj. During the walk one man died and two women give birth.[15]

One eyewitness told Maggie O'Kane of 'The Guardian' that he saw ten cattle wagons full of women and children at Trnopolje railway station, screaming for water, when the charity organisation 'Merhamet' got to them two days later, they were still screaming for water and two children had died.[16]

On 7 July 1992, seventy-five men were packed into a truck for the drive to Manjaca from Sanski Most, after already under going captivity in the town. After traveling forty miles and eight hours later, twenty were already dead. Part of the reason was that they had been sick, beaten, dehydrated and also because they were packed into a truck not capable of holding forty people let alone seventy-five and to make matters worse it was hot and there was no air.

According to one survivor, when they were ordered out of the truck, Ivan Tutic who was a young strong man: stumbled around the lorry, blood pouring from his mouth, nose and ears. The rush of fresh air when the tarpaulin was lifted must have burst every vein in his head. His was no death for a man: it was the death of a wounded beast.[17]

This was only an example of the manner in which the people were transported away. People were killed in whole groups, their bodies were piled into mass graves, or burnt. Some were not fortunate enough to die before being set alight. Thousands were put through horrendous acts of mental and physical torture.

Borislav Herak, a prisoner of war confessed to his crimes and testified that once in a field near Vogosca, 150 men, women and children were massacred and their corpses were burnt. He also stated how twenty men from Donja Bioca were incinerated, many alive. He further testified that on one occasion sixty men were killed after being used as shields for Serbian forces, which was no isolated case.[18] Another Serbian soldier testified of killing 100 people and stated that he used to cut off the ears of Muslims and sell them to Serbs for 50 German Marks each.[19]

Abzija Meduserjac, a fifty-one year old widow, who says that she now only lives to bear witness to the atrocities committed by a group of Serbian mercenaries known as the 'White Eagles' in Vishegrad, in May 1992, describes her feelings when she saw 300 people placed in a mosque and set alight, "I'll never forget their cries of terror and the smell of burnt flesh." And described a girl who escaped a burning house as a "ghost or skeleton. . . . no skin, no hair."[20]

Many in Vishegrad were tortured before they were killed, as was her neighbour Ahmed Karacik. The mercenaries put a butcher's hook down his throat and tied him to the back of a car and dragged him through the streets, so that other people could "see him and hear his cries," Abzija explained. Before his body was disposed of in the river, he was beheaded and his head was used as a football. The arms of another acquaintance, Hasan Brko, were chopped off and he was forced to drink his own blood. His end fate was similar to Ahmed's.[21]

These practices were not ad hoc but were part of the overall Serbian strategy. The aim of which was to terrorise the people into fleeing Bosnia before the same befell them, and it must be said that they were successful in their aim. Atrocities of this kind were not limited to men, being female, a child, or even a baby gave no immunity.

In a basement in Vropolje where a group of twelve women and thirty children were staying, only one women and a teenager were spared. The children were as young as four and six years.[22] In another village Zaklopaca, Serbs went into a house and killed seven people including a one year old child.[23] Abzija Meduserjac herself was forced to put the barrel of a gun down the throat of her son and was beaten when she refused to pull the trigger. She was unable to speak for eight days. According to Jose Maria Mandiluce, a former high ranker in the United Nations High Commission for Refugees (UNHCR) in the city of Zvornik children were put under the wheels of tanks and crushed.[24]

The Serbs systematically killed all Muslim leaders, intellectuals, businessmen and professionals in an aim to make the Muslims into a huge mass of refugees, unable to make any demands or to regenerate any type of power.[25] Apart from a few thousand middle class refugees who escaped to Zagreb, and few others who made it to safety elsewhere, the Muslim professional classes of Bosanska Krajina are no more.[26] On 6 April 1992, in Bijeljina, all members of the Party for Democratic Action (SDA) of Bijeljina were killed except three members of the executive committee.[27] Michael Nicholson has termed this 'elitocide'.[28]

As well as mental and physical torture a great number of women in Bosnia were also put through the ordeal of rape, often not just once or by one person. According to Bell Fialkoff between 30,000 and 50,000 (mostly) Muslim women were raped in Bosnia,[29] and according to the Sarajevo State Commission for Investigation of War Crimes, 50,000 women were raped by October 1992.[30] These figures are debatable and arriving at an exact number is almost impossible for these women have been through the traumas of war, often losing whole families, maybe even seeing them being killed. Many may have husbands, sons or other members of families in concentration camps or their whereabouts is unknown. Such women have very little concern of seeing their rapists or war criminals go on trial, and very rarely would they be willing to speak out or testify for the fear of further endangering the life of their loved ones. This is on top of shame, humility and guilt women in Bosnia feel and endure because of the act.

Prior to this brutal war, in conflicts and wars world-wide women have suffered and have been subjected to rape. One would say this is the case in majority of the wars and in many of them women have been raped to further wound the enemy and to show one's superiority. However, the rape of Muslim women in Bosnia-Herzegovina was carried out with a clear political purpose and was not just a soldiers act. Dr. Melika Kreitmayer, chief of the rape study group of the Tuzla Hospital Gynaecological Institute, who examined many rape victims stated, "these women were raped not because it was the male instinct. They were raped because it was the goal of the war".31 The women of Bosnia Herzegovina were systematically raped with orders from the highest rank of Serbian authority. It was used to cleanse Bosnia-Herzegovina of Muslim women. Organised rape, was part of the Serbian grand policy of ethnic cleansing. Many soldiers told their victims that they were only doing it because they had to, and some with a bit of conscience actually let their victims go with the instructions to pretend they were raped. Men were killed or put into camps and the women were raped and the majority of whom were impregnated, thus also threatening the potential of reproduction. Often women were kept in captivity until it was not possible to have an abortion.32 One women was told by her tormentor that they wanted to "plant the seeds of Serbs in Bosnia."33

This further added to the fear of women, and those that had as yet not been subjected to this brutality hastened to flee the area. Using this hideous practice to cleanse Bosnia-Herzegovina of Muslims seems all the more successful when we try to gauge the feelings and views of the victims. Senada, a seventeen year old rape victim in her statement wrote, "It is worse then any other punishment in the world."34 Many victims stated that instead of Bosnia they would rather be anywhere else in the world, and once the war was over they would leave, never to return.35 Often than not the victims would say that they would never be able to partake in the act of sexual intercourse ever again.36 The tales of practices from victims and witnesses; the manner ferocity and brutality with which they were carried out, is incomprehensible to the sound mind.

A group of forty women from Brezovo Polje were raped and according to the gynaecological team that later examined them, "most had vaginal infections", and all but one had been virgins.37 In the village of Liplje, according to Dr. Kreitmayer practically every women was raped.38 Very often rape was used to humiliate the people involved. One woman, Almira was raped for five nights by three men each night. On the sixth night her father was forced to watch.39 Enes Caric writes how one woman was raped in front of her children, parents and husband:

The general said: 'rape her first before the eyes of those whom she bore, then before the eyes of those who bore her, then before the eyes of her husband who fathered children with her.'40

In a village near Prijedor, a fourteen year old girl was tied naked to a tank and driven around the village. After being raped and half dead she was thrown in front of her parents.41 Age or condition of the victims did not deter the Serbs, for there is even an incident of a retarted girl being raped.42 One fifty-seven year old woman was raped, not once but twenty times,43 and one child, Samira, who was born in 1989 was in Tuzla hospital by March 1993, after being raped. She had trouble urinating and had a broken hymen. The mother who herself was also raped stated that when she was allowed to go and take Samira, "her head was blue and she had foam on her mouth."44

Many rape camps were established by the Serbs. A leading Bosnian women group estimated that in August 1992 10,000 women were being held in concentration camps or detention centres where they were repeatedly raped.45 The Partizan sports hall, in Foca was one such centre. One woman prisoner of the centre claimed that she had been raped more than 100 times. Examination by a gynaecologist after her release confirmed her story to be credible.46 Another woman was raped 150 times.47 But the sad part of their tale was that they were no exceptions. There are also a huge number of reports of gang rapes.48

Beside these 'centres' for women the Serbs also established camps in which most of the men, usually excepting the old, were sent. According to the Bosnian government within four months of the war, the Serbs had established fifty-seven camps in which 147,000 people were being held. Most were Muslims, some Croat and some were even disloyal Serbs. An iron mine and ore processing works at Omarska was turned into a death camp, although the Serbs called them 'transit centres'. According to US government officials out of a total 13,000 people processed at Omarska 5,000 were killed.49 According to the Bosnian State Commission on War Crimes at a camp in Brcko, in six weeks, between May and June 1992, 3 000 people were slaughtered.50 In Bosanski Samac, various buildings including schools and a police station were turned into detention centres for civilians, where an estimated 800 people were held. Although the Serbs claimed that no camps existed for civilians, those people who emerged from such centres had broken bones and damaged organs. Survivors told stories of being beaten with iron bars, truncheons and baseball bats over the head, neck, back, chest, feet, legs, arms and lips; practically all over the body.51 Such treatment was standard all over Bosnia. At Omarska there was even an open air pit, 1000 feet deep, in which 500-1000 prisoners were made to lie on their stomachs from morning to night.52 ITN reporters visited Omarska and describe what they saw:

The men are at various stages of human decay and affliction; the bones of their elbows and wrists protrude like pieces of jagged stone from the pencil-thin stalks to which their arms have been reduced. Their skin is putrified, the complexion of their faces have been corroded. These humans are alive but decomposed, debased, degraded, and utterly subservient, and yet they fix their huge, hollow eyes on us with looks like the blades of knives.53

At Trnopolje camp in one incident, 200 people were shot and thrown into a ravine.54 At another camp, Kereterm, during one night, gas bombs were thrown into a large room of prisoners, those that fled to the door were then gunned down. Witnesses estimate that 125 people were killed and another 45 were injured.55 On one occasion at Omarska 150 prisoners were kept without food and water for four days, and then a single canister of water was put between them, to make them fight.56

Bodies were often mutilated as one survivor from Brcko said, "I saw it with my own eyes. . . . ten young men laid in a row. They had their throats slit, their noses cut off and genitals plucked out."57 The bodies were even cremated for animal feed.58 At the Luka camp, prisoners were taken out one by one and dogs which had not eaten for days were set on them.59 At the Kereterm camp, one prisoner's ear was cut off and another was forced to eat it.60

All this was on top of the harsh living conditions, very little food and very poor sanitation which the prisoners had to endure. Prisoners preferred to excrete in their boots rather than going to the toilet for the fear of beatings.61 They were so crowded that one prisoner explained, "there was nowhere to lie down. You'd drowse off and fall against the next person".62 Another explained, "You could not put your foot down without treading on someone's foot, hand or head".63

But the worst and most traumatic for the prisoners were castrations, which was not unusual. One witness told US embassy officials of an incident in which a wire was tied around a man's testicles and then to a motorbike, which then moved off at high speed. The prisoner died due to loss of blood.64 At the Hague war crimes tribunal, a survivor from Omarska, Halid Mujkanovic testified that a fellow prisoner was forced to perform fellatio upon another prisoner, Fikret Harambasic, and was then forced to bite off his genitals. His refusal would have cost the lives of his other room mates. All along the guards looked on as if watching "a sports match, supporting a team", said Halid.65 It seems there was no end to the perverse cruelty displayed at the camps. In one detention centre the barbarity was such that holes were drilled into the chests of three children aged 1, 3, and 5 and were then impaled on spikes.66

At the camps the leading political, academic and professional people were listed and singled out for persecution. Just to give an example, on 8 November 1992, the names of seven men were called out; six Muslims, one Croat. One was an elected lord mayor of a city, two were gynaecologists, one was a state prosecutor, another owned a cafe and an art gallery and there were two others. They were never seen alive again, although many saw their corpses in a nearby field the next day.67 Another such incident took place on 26 and 27 July 1992, when fifty names were called out, amongst them were judges, civil servants, surgeons, businessmen and teachers.

In short, "all the prominent people of Prijedor", as one witness explained.68 But the elite of Prijedor were not an exception but, "all the prominent people at Omarska," were killed, as clarified by a survivor.69 This was also the case for women. An ethnic Croat Jadrunka Cigelj, a lawyer and political activist, was taken to Omarsca. In the administration room she was joined by three other lawyers, two economists, four teachers, two doctors, one dentist, one electrical engineer, one metallurgical engineer, one nurse, two with college degrees in economics and the rest high school graduates. Two were Croats, and the rest Muslims.70

The atrocities and cleansing was not limited to humans but Serbs endeavoured to obliterate a whole culture. More than 800 Bosnian mosques have been totally or in part destroyed. The oldest mosque in

Bosnia the Emin Turhan Bey Mosque at Ustikolina built in 1448/9 is no more. In Visegrad in the place of the Imperial mosque now stands the 'Serbian Cultural Centre'. The mosque in Modrica was turned into a slaughterhouse for pigs. In Sarajevo the Institute for Oriental Studies has been blown away, and most of its thousands of documents and manuscripts have been lost including important historical documents of Ottoman Bosnia, like original Berats (Sultan's Edicts), land ownership certificates etc. Clearly a cultural genocide has taken place.71

There is no doubt that ethnic cleaning of the Muslims did take place in Bosnia-Herzegovina. But many journalists, politicians and academics have claimed that genocide did not. One observer has argued that there was no genocide because the number of victims was low. But this argument is baseless, for there is no threshold for genocide.72 Having a very large number of victims is not a criteria for genocide. Many have argued that calling the atrocities committed in Bosnia genocide would make light of the German Holocaust and would take-away its horrors and severity. However, if we accept this then we would be making light of not only the Bosnian tragedy but also all other such horrors (if they were to occur) in the future. For no matter how great the tragedy they would not be regarded so bad, because they could not be called genocide. Also terming something genocide, does not have to take away any significance from the German Holocaust. Another theorist has argued that "ethnic cleansing while indefensible, is not genocide". Although this may be true in some cases, it is not so in the case of Bosnia.73 As Theodor Meron has pointed out, the systematic nature of mass murders and ethnic cleansing in Bosnia puts those atrocities under the category of 'crimes against humanity', and because it was directed against a religious or ethnic group, it is a "strong case for genocide".74

Also, in his address to the UN Security Council, Diego Arria, Venezuela's Ambassador to the UN reminded them that, "the International Court of Justice and the World Conference on Human Rights both have indicated that Bosnia-Herzegovina is a victim of genocide and "ethnic cleansing", among other unspeakable crimes."75

References for Chapter One :

1. Andrew Bell-Fialkoff, Ethnic Cleansing, London: Macmillan, 1996, p. 3
2. Philip J. Cohen, 'Ending the War and Securing Peace in Former Yugoslavia', In Stjepan G. Mestrovic (ed), Genocide After Emotion. The Postemotional Balkan War, London: Routledge, 1996, p. 31
3. Christopher Bennett, Yugoslavia's Bloody Collapse. Causes, Course and Consequences, London: Hurst & Company, 1995, p. 1
4. Mujeeb R. Khan, 'Bosnia-Herzegovina and the Crisis of the Post-Cold War International System', in East European Politics and Societies, Vol. 9, No. 3, p. 461
5. Theodor Meron, 'The Case for War Crimes Trials in Yugoslavia', in Foreign Affairs, Vol. 72, No. 3, p. 132
6. The United Nations and Human Rights 1945-1995, The United Nations Blue Book Series, Vol. 7, p.

424

7. ibid., p. 151
8. Roy Gutman, A witness to Genocide, Shaftesbury: Element, 1993, p. xxxi
9. Norman Cigar, Genocide in Bosnia. The Policy of Ethnic Cleansing, College Station: Texas A & M University Press, 1995, p. 9
10. The New York Times, 9 March 1995, cited in Stjepan G. Mestrovic (ed), Genocide After Emotion. The Postemotional Balkan War, London: Routledge, 1996, p. 1
11. cited in Stjepan G. Mestrovic (ed), Genocide After Emotion. The Postemotional Balkan War, London: Routledge, 1996, p. 7
12. David Rieff, Slaughterhouse. Bosnia and the Failure of the West, London: Vintage, 1995, p. 17
13. ibid.
14. Ed Vulliamy, Seasons in Hell. Understanding Bosnia's War, London: Simon and Schnster, 1994, pp. 91-92
15. Gutman, op. cit., p.40
16. The Guardian, 29 July 1992, cited in Vulliamy, op. cit., p. 96
17. Orphan Bosnevic, The Road to Manjaca, In Rabia Ali and Lawrence Lifschultz (eds), Why Bosnia? Writings on the Balkan War, Stony Creek: The pamphleteer's Press Inc., 1993, p. 107
18. Vulliamy, op. cit., p. 193
19. The Daily Jang, London, 7 November 1997
20. Juan Goytisolo, 'Torture Town', in New Statesman and Society, 17/31 December 1993, p. 48
21. ibid., p. 47
22. Vulliamy, op. cit., p. 142
23. Ibrahim Kajan, Is This Not Genocide? In Rabia Ali and Lawrence Lifschultz (eds), Why Bosnia? Writings on the Balkan War, Stony Creek: The pamphleteer's Press Inc., 1993, p. 94
24. Goytisolo, op. cit., pp. 47-48
25. Marko Prelek, The Western Response to the War in Bosnia. A House Built on Sand. In Rabia Ali and Lawrence Lifschultz (eds), Why Bosnia? Writings on the Balkan War, Stony Creek: The pamphleteer's Press Inc., 1993, p. 193
26. Rieff, op. cit., p. 113
27. Kajan, op. cit., p. 87
28. Rieff, op. cit.
29. Bell-Fialkoff, op. cit., p. 47
30. Slavenka Draculic, Women Hide Behind a Wall of Silence. In Rabia Ali and Lawrence Lifschultz (eds), Why Bosnia? Writings on the Balkan War, Stony Creek: The pamphleteer's Press Inc., 1993, p. 118
31. Gutman, op. cit., p. 69
32. Draculic, op. cit., p. 119
33. Gutman, op. cit., p. 76
34. ibid., p. 69
35. ibid., p. 73
36. ibid., p. 76
37. ibid., p. 71
38. ibid., p. 74
39. ibid.,
40. Enes Caric, The Land of Inexhaustible Inspiration. In Rabia Ali and Lawrence Lifschultz (eds), Why Bosnia? Writings on the Balkan War, Stony Creek: The pamphleteer's Press Inc., 1993, p. 123
41. Vulliamy, op. cit., p. 200
42. Kajan, op. cit., p. 95
43. Gutman, op. cit., p. 76
44. Vulliamy, op. cit., p. 196
45. Gutman, op. cit., p. 169
46. ibid., p. 164
47. ibid., p. 166
48. ibid., p. 64
49. ibid., p. xiv
50. ibid., p. 50

51. ibid., p. 56
52. ibid., p. 62 & p. 90
53. Vulliamy, op. cit., p. 102
54. Gutman, op. cit., p. 85
55. ibid., p. 84.
56. Vulliamy, op. cit., p.110
57. Gutman, op. cit., p. 51
58. ibid., p. 50
59. Vulliamy op. cit., p. 113
60. Gutman, op. cit., p. 98
61. ibid., p. 100
62. ibid., p. 48
63. The Observer, 28 July 1996.
64. Gutman, op. cit., p. 98
65. The Observer, 28 July 1996.
66. Gutman, op. cit., p. 41
67. ibid., p. 109
68. ibid.
69. ibid., p. 110
70. ibid., p. 147
71. Vulliamy, op. Cit., pp. 353-354
72. Cigar, op. cit., pp.116-117
73. ibid., p. 116
74. Meron, op. Cit., p.130
75. Raba Ali & Lawrence Lifschultz (eds), Why Bosnia? Writings on the Balkan War,Stony Creek: The Pamphleteer's Press, Inc., 1993, p xxix

CHAPTER TWO
THE INTERNATIONAL COMMUNITY: THE PLAYERS

In November 1991, Alija Izetbegovic warned of the threat of war breaking out in Bosnia- Herzegovina, and requested United Nations peacekeeping forces to stop the tragedy before it actually happened. The request was repeated in December 1991 but nothing was done. As predicted war broke out and after two months on May 30th the international community took its first piece of action and imposed trade sanctions on Serbia.1 This was in addition to the arms embargo imposed on all the states of former Yugoslavia since September 1991 by the US, EC and a little later by the UN.2 Izetbegovic who all the time showed his commitment to peace and the desire to avoid disintegration expected the international powers to intervene, but this was not to happen.

As the war broke out the Bosnian government and even the people of the world expected various actors in the international community to intervene. One such was the only super power of the world i.e. the United States. Another was the European Community and its member states for whom the crisis was on their doorstep. The next was the United Nations, which was expected to help maintain peace in the world. In this chapter I will look at each of these in turn, at their actions and what affected them.

UNITED STATES
One may ask why the leading power of the world, which was able to bring together the major nations of the world to liberate Kuwait from Iraqi occupation took a half-hearted approach, rather than a leading role in the Bosnian tragedy. Various answers and reasons can be given but they all come back in the end to the term 'national interest' or lack of it. As Warren Christopher declared in July 1993, that Bosnia is of no "vital interest" to America.3

At the onset of war in Bosnia, the US was no longer engaged in the Cold War but was in the process of furthering relationships with the Soviet government, which had close ties with the Serbs. Geographically, the Balkans also was of no great importance to the United States for the threat from the Soviet Union (as mentioned) no longer existed. As President Clinton allegedly said to some journalists, "see this Bosnia thing in the context of everything else that's going on in the world, including Russia."4 No major economic interests were at stake either. The US did wish to maintain ties with its NATO allies without becoming involved too much and without seeming to interfere. Therefore, the lead was given to the European Community (EC) for whom the stakes were greater and was closer to home. It is true that international principles and laws were being violated, thousands of innocent human lives were being lost and human rights were being abused, but these interests did not outweigh America's own interests, the costs and the risks to the American servicemen. The unimportance of Bosnia in the eyes of President Bush can be gauged by his statement, "I don't think anybody suggests that that if there is a hiccup here or there that the United States is going to send troops".5 As long as pressure from the electorate did not coerce the government, humanitarian interests or principles itself would not alter the policy. Politicians argued that if the US intervened and sent troops it would become another Vietnam. Chairman of the joint chiefs of staff, General Colin Powell, who was against the deployment of troops argued that hundreds of thousands of troops would be required. Arther Schlesinger is alleged to have warned President Clinton that involvement in Bosnia "could destroy his domestic hopes as surely as Vietnam destroyed Lyndon Johnsons's Great Society".6

From the very beginning the aim of the US and the EC had been to contain the conflict and to prevent a spillover. The desk officer for Yugoslavia, George Kenney (who resigned during the Bush administration) allegedly asserted that, "virtually all the staff working on these issues agree that our Balkan policy is a total failure. . . . [and] that American policy borders on complicity in genocide".7 Thus the US policy was limited to containing the conflict and preventing it from spilling over into other areas such as Kosovo and Macedonia which would then involve Greece, Albania, Turkey and possibly extend even further. For this reason, the UN Secretary General, in 1992 recommended the deployment of UNPROFOR along the Macedonian border with Serbia and Albania.8 To highlight this further in 1993, Warren Christopher allegedly said, "we have to save our power for those situations which threaten our deepest national interests".9

One reason given for the slack approach by the US is the bias of Lawrence Eagleburger and Brent Scowcroft towards Serbia, Eagleburger had been an ambassador to Yugoslavia and Scowcroft also had connections with the embassy in Belgrade. Both had long standing diplomatic, business and personal connections in Belgrade.10

Throughout the crisis the US played a two-track game. It can be put down to just inconsistency or if it wasn't inconsistency then it was deceit, contempt and a true bias towards the Serbs. Although the US called for air strikes and lifting of the arms embargo, originally when in 1991, the EC lifted economic sanctions from all the republican states, except Serbia and Montenegro, the US just a few days later imposed sanctions on all the republics.11 Even when the US was condemning Serb aggression, it was training its personnel in America. Major Getrovic of the Yugoslav army spent ten months training in the US before returning back to the war.12

EUROPEAN COMMUNITY

The European Community, generally wished to use the Bosnian war to advance integration in matters of defence and security. It gave the individual member states an opportunity to come together and to show that they can act as one, cohesively. In 1990, America's offer of assistance and consultation was declined, and it was even accused by the French of "over-dramatising the situation". Luxembourg's foreign minister captured the fervour when he talked of "the hour of Europe".13 However, it soon became apparent that they were not united, but as with the United States, the action of the European nations was also determined by the issue of national or strategic interests, and each member state was giving priority to its own national interest, and were looking at the issue from their own perspective. Without vital interests being at stake no country was willing to risk lives of soldiers for other people's problems.

Steven Burg has argued that the conflict may have been left for the Europeans to handle by the United States, precisely for the reason that their internal divisions and differences meant they would fail in the task, pointing to the need for American leadership in issues of security in Europe.14

Germany initially used the war to show its authority on the international scene, to show it was on par with other nations, and to gain more flexibility. This was the motive behind Genscher's recognition of Slovenia and Croatia. But when this did not stop the war Germany had no answer, and although it called for military intervention claimed that its constitution forbade intervention outside the NATO area, which further irritated other members.15   However, even after a constitutional ruling allowed Germany to intervene military, it did not.16 The war also coincided with a new era for Germany. The German Democratic Republic (GDR) had collapsed in 1989 and the two German states became one in 1990. Thus at the time, attention was fully upon internal problems. In 1993, after the Geneva peace talks, due to pressure from public opinion the German government called for the lifting of the arms embargo, but was not willing to act unilaterally.17

This left two major powers, France and the United Kingdom (UK). France even before the war, was in favour of Europe taking a stronger role in the field of defense and security, but when nothing of real significance was achieved through the EC, it further pursued its objectives through the corridors of the UN. This gave France the additional benefit of Germany not being present and of France having an authoritative voice in all matters through the Security Council, if matters involved NATO.18

It can also be said that France took an approach biased towards the Serbs, or at least conciliatory. Originally, France was not willing to blame Serbia for the outbreak of war, and only after a year of aggression did Mitterand recognise Serbia's role and responsibility.19 Mitterand was also trying to preserve the historical friendship between Serbia and France, which according to Mitterand's statement while welcoming Prime Minister Ante Marcovic had existed, since "the Napoleonic era and reinforced by the two world wars".20 As argued by Oliver Lepick, this also gave France an opportunity to act as an intermediary between Serbia and the rest of the world. If France was successful Serbia would be grateful and France would have an influence upon the region, as well as establishing for itself an important position in international security issues.21

Britain viewed Bosnia as another Northern Ireland and with no national interests at stake did not want to become involved, but still did take a leading diplomatic role.22 At the onset of war, attention of the government in Britain and the other politicians was focused upon the oncoming General Election.

UNITED NATIONS
The UN has come under considerable criticism for its role in Bosnia and has lost a lot of credibility. Many scholars have pointed to the fact that NATO and UN, two distinct bodies were trying to manage the conflict which hindered the ability to reach key decisions. However, this is only an excuse which has no weight, for the UN and NATO are only that which the member states wish to make of it. The key players in NATO and those in the UN are more or less the same. These institutions are vulnerable to the powerful member states. As Mohamed Sacirbey, Bosnia's Ambassador to the UN said, "the UN has been hijacked. . . . by the very countries that have the greatest responsibility for its future."23 And according to Tadeusz Mazowiecki, "the UN has become a convenient whipping boy.

Decisions are taken not by the UN but by its member states."24

The UN is criticised for not acting early enough when Izetbegovic requested troops, which could have prevented the war from occurring. Inaction after the London Conference told the Serbs there would be no intervention.25
A major mistake has been to send peacekeeping forces into a war torn area. Peacekeepers need to remain neutral, have the consent of the parties involved, carry very little arms and use force only in self-defense. Peacekeeping is a "non-military mission carried out by military personnel".26 In Bosnia peacekeeping forces were not sent when there was peace to be kept, but were sent after war broke out, and there was no peace to be kept. By sending peacekeeping forces where peace enforcement forces were needed the UN became very vulnerable. The Bosnian government as the rightful government of Bosnia and a member of the UN, expected the UN to protect its borders and sovereignty from outside aggression, but the mandate of the peacekeepers on the ground meant they were mere observers. The UN in Bosnia, as described by Sacirbey were "nothing more than observers and truck drivers".27

What is clear is that the appropriate mandate was not applied to Bosnia. Serbia is the clear aggressor and Chapter 7 of the UN Charter which deals with aggressors states that all necessary means have to be taken until the aggressor is punished and the aggression is reversed. But this is peace enforcement, not peacekeeping which is dealt with by Chapter 6 of the Charter.28

Tadeusz Mazowiecki, Special Rapporteur of the United Nations' Commission on the former Yugoslavia, resigned from his position and in his letter of resignation wrote, "In my view the UNPROFOR mandate was essentially sick. It was assumed that it was possible to go into a war situation with a peacekeeping mandate".29

The UN troops on the ground have also come under criticism. The mandate again is partly to blame, for atrocities were taking place and the UN stood and watched. They were under no obligation to do anything. As Mazowiecki complained, they were not even under the:
obligation to pass on documentation relating to human rights abuses. There was one occasion when vital information concerning a serious war crime (the mass graves at Ovcara near Vukovar) was not communicated to us.30

General, Lewis Mackenzie initially Chief of staff to UNPROFOR (Croatia) and later Commander of sector Sarajevo has allegedly been accused of being biased towards the Serbs. This view was given credibility when it emerged that after leaving Bosnia he went on a speaking tour paid by the group SerbNet, (Serbian American National Information Network) in which he gave speeches and interviews with CNN, Time magazine, Washington Times and ABC radio amongst others. He argued against US military intervention and also stated that the majority of ceasefire violations in Bosnia were committed by Muslims. Although other officers who served with him say this is not true.31

General Sir Micheal Rose has also come in for considerable criticism. Even officers close to him allegedly say he was sympathetic towards the Serb position.32 He accused the Muslims of ethnically cleansing 12,500 Serbs from Gorazde, for which there is no evidence.33 He was also strictly against the use of force. During the air assault on Bihac the pilots were under strict rules of identifying smoking guns before they could strike. SAS teams in radio contact with Sir Michael Rose were responsible for locating the guns. NATO planes took off from Italy but Sir Michael Rose allegedly ordered the SAS not to identify the target.

Within days Serb tanks were clearing their way through the suburbs of Bihac.34 Sir Michael Rose even went a step further and gave detailed NATO flight plans to the Serbs.35 The MP Calum Macdonald has also allegedly accused him of accepting two oil paintings from the Serbs. Why they were given, one can only guess.36

UN soldiers from France, New Zealand, Ukraine and Canada are alleged to have repeatedly visited Sonja's kon-Tiki café, a brothel of women prisoners, and even killing two. However, UN investigations found no evidence of anything untoward.

There was also a considerable problem with the Russian contingent in the UN force. During one cease-fire the keys to the storage area where Serbian weapons were kept were given by a Russian Soldier to the Serbs, allowing them to take fifty-one tanks.37 Thus, it can be said that the UN did as the Major powers desired, there were problems with its mandate, its commanding officers and also some of its ground troops.

References for Chapter Two

1. Sabrina Petra Ramet, 'The Bosnian War and the Diplomacy of Accommodation', in Current History, Vol. 93, No. 586, p. 381
2. Philip J. Cohen, 'Ending the War and Securing Peace in Former Yugoslavia', In Stjepan G. Mestrovic (ed), Genocide After Emotion. The Post Emotional Balkan War, London: Routledge, 1996, p. 32
3. Rabia Ali and Lawrence Lifschultz (eds), Why Bosnia? Writings on the Bulkan War, Stony Creek, The Pamphleteer's Press, 1993, p. xl
4. ibid, p. xlii
5. Sabrina Petra Ramet, 'The Yugoslav Crisis and the West: Avoiding "Vietnam" and Blundering into "Abyssinia", in East European Politics and Societies, Vol. 8 No. 1, p. 205

6. Ali and Lifschultz (eds) op. cit., p. xxxviii

7. ibid., p. xli

8. Susan L. Woodward, Balkan Tragedy. Choas and Dissolution After the Cold War, Washington: The Brookings Institution, 1995, p. 295

9. Roy Gutman, A witness to Genocide, Shaftesbury: Element, 1993, p. xli

10. Cohen, op. cit., p. 40

11. ibid., p. 39

12. ibid., p. 41 & p. 50

13. David Gompert, 'How to Defeat Serbia' in Foreign Affairs, Vol. 73, No. 4, p. 35

14. Steven L. Burg, 'Why Yugoslavia Fell Apart' in Current History, Vol. 92, No. 577, p. 362

15. Gerd Koslowski, 'Bosnia: Failure of the Institutions and of the Balance of Power in Europe, in Aussenpolitik, Vol. 47, No. 4 , p. 361

16. Marie-Janine Calic in Alex Danchev and Thomas Halverson (eds), International Perspectives on the Yugoslav Conflict, London: Macmillan Press Ltd., 1996, p. 65

17. ibid., p. 52

18. Koslowski, op. cit., p. 362

19. Calic, op. cit., p. 78

20. ibid.

21. ibid.

22. ibid., p. 90

23. Mohamed Sacirbey, 'End of the Line. An Open Letter to the British Public', in New Statesman and Society, 28 July 1995, p. 14

24. Tadeusz Mazowiecki, 'Will to Disaster', in Index on censorship, Vol., 24, No. 5, p. 71

25. Gompert, op. cit., p. 38

26. John Gerard Ruggie, 'Wandering in the Void. Charting the UN's New Strategic Role, in Foreign Affairs, Vol. 72, No. 5, p. 28

27. Sacirbey, op. cit., p. 75

28. ibid.

29. Mazowieki, op. cit., p. 71

30. ibid., p. 70

31. Gutman, op. cit., p. 170

32. Roger Cohen, The New York Times, 25 September 1994, cited in Mestrovic (ed), op. cit., p. 208

33. Calum Macdonald, 'Rose-tinted Spectacles', in New Statesman and Society, 10 February 1995, p. 23

34. The Guardian, 29 January 1996.

35. Macdonald, op. cit.

36. The Guardian, 24 February 1995.

37. Dale Van Atta, 'The Folly of UN Peacekeeping', in Reader's Digest, October 1995, p. 120

CHAPTER THREE

THE INTERNATIONAL COMMUNITY: THE RESPONSE

MILITARY INTERVENTION.

As the war progressed the international community had the option of pursuing one of a few policies. They could either have intervened militarily with ground forces, or use air strikes against the Serbs without ground forces. If not, they could have removed the arms embargo (imposed upon all of the republics of the former Yugoslavia) and let the Muslims arm and defend themselves. Another possibility was to demilitarise certain towns and declare them safe areas, under UN observation, which the international community did. In this chapter I will look at each of these possibilities separately.

Political theorists against the idea of military intervention argued that it would cause more bloodshed and would also endanger the lives of peace keeping forces, as was argued by Britain and France all along. They also argued that to achieve success in separating the warring factions such a large force would be needed that the major powers just would not be in a position to provide it. The American army was 25% smaller than it was during the Gulf war and even that was deployed in Somalia, Saudi Arabia and Kuwait. Britain's army was in a similar position, with troops posted in Northern Ireland, Hong Kong, Falklands, Cyprus, Brunei and Belize. France although has a large army, in order to deploy a reasonable force would have had to raise the numbers from its conscript army. As mentioned earlier, Germany was restricted by its constitution. Whereas the Italians and Spanish armies are undergoing such cutbacks that they no longer are a major force, in a position to give a reasonable amount of troops.1

Even so, the truth of the matter is that this is only an excuse to justify inaction. If national or strategic interests were at stake, the troops would have been available and military intervention would have occurred. The politicians nonetheless realised that nothing less than a military intervention would stop the Serbs, as Jacques Delors told the European Parliament.2 Even Douglas Hurd who was strongly opposed to any sort of intervention felt obligated to acknowledge that "the only thing, which could have guaranteed peace with justice, would have been an expeditionary force".3

AIR STRIKES
The Clinton administration wanted to use air strikes but the British and French objected due to the forces on the ground. Later France did approve but Britain remained opposed. Lord Owen taunted America with the words, "you will not achieve anything at 10,000 feet",4 because the US were pushing for air strikes but were not willing to send in ground troops where the risk lay. Throughout the conflict Britain remained the strongest advocate of non-intervention. James Gow writes, "Hurd and the British government were backwards in coming forwards. . . . Hurd reacted swiftly to subdue discussion of using force whenever the issue arose".

After the Market Square bombing on 5 February 1994, there was a public outcry which caused the US to push for NATO intervention and air strikes. The US also argued that the legal authority for military action already existed within the UN Security Council Resolutions. The French also were in favour of NATO intervention. On 9 February 1994, in a NATO council meeting both the US and France were in favour of issuing a NATO ultimatum, but Britain alone opposed. At the time General Rose was working to reach an agreement between the parties involved. But even though at the time of the meeting nothing had been achieved, a British representative claimed that General Rose had secured an agreement of demilitarisation, thus forestalling intervention.5

Lord Owen and Britain did not want NATO to act independently, but with the UN. Lord Owen knew that the Russians would side with the Serbs and would oppose intervention. If NATO acted independently of the UN then the Russians would not be included in the decision making and intervention would take place. This Owen believed would lead to Russia aligning with the Serbs and NATO with the Muslims.6 Thus, Britain made sure military action against the Serbs did not take place, regardless of the consequences to the Muslims.

NATO, nevertheless still issued an ultimatum and all heavy weapons had to be moved 20 km away from the city centre or be under UN control. General Rose asked for all heavy weapons to be placed at the airport, because it was the only neutral ground, but the Serbs refused. They even refused to place them at five other points proposed by General Rose. Eventually the Serbs were allowed to choose. They chose three positions inside the city and five outside. However, according to the Bosnian government they were the very strategic positions from where the city had been shelled for almost two years. Thus, with the aid of Britain and especially General Rose, air strikes had been avoided but the siege of Sarajevo continued.7 General Rose and his actions also led to a dispute between NATO and UN over the word 'control'. For General Rose did not have control over the weapons, they were only under his supervision. NATO stressed taking control of the weapons was necessary and General Rose argued supervision was enough. With the Serbs not willing to hand over any weapons, NATO intervention seemed likely. That is until John Major stepped in and decided to visit President Yeltsin. He agreed with President Yeltsin that the West would not act without Russia's consent in the future. This led to President Yeltsin sending a letter to the Serbs telling them to hand over the weapons and guaranteeing them that Russian troops would move into the areas from which they would withdraw. Thus again, with the aid of Britain air strikes were blocked but the siege continued and the positioning of UN troops meant Sarajevo was divided; a key Serb war aim,8 as Karadzic had revealed earlier in an interview with Warren Zimmerman, "the city will be divided with Muslim, Serbian and Croatian sections, so that no ethnic groups will have to live or work together. . . . Our vision of Sarajevo is like Berlin when the wall was still standing".9 In the end only a few symbolic air raids took place which only helped to undermine NATO's credibility.

ARMS EMBARGO

The world powers were not willing to intervene, send in ground troops, or use credible air strikes. Thus, the only credible option remaining was to allow the Muslims to defend themselves by lifting the arms embargo. The arms embargo clearly advantaged the Serbs who had the bulk of the weapons of the Yugoslav People's Army (JNA) and also controlled most of the defense industry. To show his peaceful intentions before the outbreak of war, Izetbegovic had allowed the JNA to disarm the republic's territorial defense units and confiscate all weapons, when at the same time weapons were being distributed among Serb militias.10 One could say he was naïve. In addition to this, the Yugoslav army had purchased an extra 14,000 tons of weapons from the Middle East just before the arms embargo was applied.11 In comparison, according to Mark Thompson, "when the assault was already under way" the Bosnian government which was defending Bosnia from Serbian aggression, "had no artillery, no tanks, no planes, no missiles."12 It was estimated that in September 1992 the Serbs in Bosnia possessed 40 aircrafts, 300 tanks, 200 armoured personnel carriers and 800 artillery pieces. Whereas the Bosnian government only had 2 tanks and 2 armoured personnel carriers. The Serbs had so much arms and ammunition that the commanders used to boast that they had enough to continue in Bosnia for Six or Seven years.13

It is when one looks at the benefits of the embargo for the Serbs, that one can understand why the Yugoslav foreign minister, Bladimir Loncar, initially called for the imposition of the arms embargo.14 The legality of the UN resolution 712 which imposes the arms embargo upon Bosnia is in itself questionable after its independence. Further to which it made an independent state, a member of the UN defenseless, although Article 51 of the UN Chapter states that all members possess this right.15 Article 51 reads:
Nothing in the present Charter shall impair the inherent right of individual and collective self-defense if an armed attack occurs against a member of the United Nations, until the Security Council has taken measures necessary to maintain international peace and security.16

Michael Scharf and Paul Wilkinson have argued that the application of the UN arms embargo upon Bosnia is a violation of international law.17 President Clinton also said, "the United Nations made a grave error by applying the arms embargo on Yugoslavia to Bosnia after they recognised Bosnia".18

Realising this harsh injustice the UN General Assembly voted by an overwhelming majority to lift the embargo and asked the Security Council for the removal of Resolution 713, but nothing was done. Venezuela, New Zealand and Pakistan, non-permanent members of the Security Council consistently called for the lifting of the arms embargo.

19 In July 1993, Diego Arria, Venezuela's Ambassador to the United Nations, addressed the Security Council and summed up their actions and behaviour, "the reality. . . . To do all that one can possibly do to prevent a people from exercising its right to defend itself in order to survive".20

The Clinton administration did call for the lifting of the embargo but UK, France and Russia opposed it. The UK argued that lifting the embargo would prolong the war and more blood would be spilt. But, whether arming the weak against the aggressor would cause more bloodshed is open to doubt. For the civilians would be defended, therefore less atrocities would be committed and less civilians would die. Having an armed force in opposition would also curb Serb ambitions of a Greater Serbia. In addition to this having a better equipped army would also mean that less civilians would be exposed to the fighting, therefore less humanitarian assistance would be needed and as a result less humanitarian aid workers would be needed and a smaller peacekeeping force would be needed to defend them. Thus, all pointing to the fact that lifting the arms embargo would not cause more bloodshed but would actually reduce the potential threat.

The aim was a quick solution and an end to the war. As was allegedly explained by Lord Owen, that lifting the arms embargo would be "disincentive to the Muslims" to negotiate', and thus would prolong the war.21

But in reality this is no excuse, for never in a war has it so happened that one side is made and kept defenseless to shorten the length of the war. If Britain in its fight against Nazi Germany was not given assistance and arms by the US the war would have had a much shorter, although unpleasant outcome.

In April 1993, Lord Owen argued that the arms embargo actually helped the Muslims for it stopped the Serbs acquiring "sophisticated armament" from the Russians.22 But, the truth is they already had all the weapons they needed and were even acquiring from Russia during the war.23 Another excuse given by those opposing the lifting of the embargo is that it would not benefit the Muslims, for if the embargo is lifted then the protection forces would have to leave. Thus, the Muslims would be slaughtered before they received any arms. However, the Muslims were being slaughtered anyway and were not protected by the UN. The UN only fired when they were themselves fired upon, not when the civilians were being shelled. Also, the decision to take that chance should rest with the Bosnian government and they clearly wished to take it.24

Britain and France also argued that lifting the embargo would jeopardise the lives of their troops on the ground. However, Mujeeb Khan, argues that during the Bihac crisis a number of Islamic countries offered to replace the British and French troops to pave the way for Clinton's 'lift and strike' policy, but both France and Britain backed down straight away.25

Not doubting that through humanitarian assistance thousands of lives were saved and relief did reach the refugee camps, but they also were a handicap for the Muslims, for the potential threat to the UN soldiers on the ground was used as a major factor for non-intervention and keeping the arms embargo.

The economic sanctions did bring pressure on the Serbian government and did affect Serbia's economy but obviously not enough to put the Serbs off war, or their ambitions of a Greater Serbia. It was no secret that fuel, strategic supplies and other goods were constantly flowing into Serbia from Italy, Ukraine, Romania, Russia, Greece, Macedonia and Albania.26 But on the other hand the sanctions did bring one benefit to the Western powers; it allowed them to say something was being done to stop the war and that Serbia was being punished. It allowed for the arms embargo to remain

Noel Malcolm believes that if the Bosnian government was allowed its right to self-defense and allowed to purchase weapons, the Serbs would have been rolled back all the way, or at least so far that they would have realised that they would not gain a Greater Serbia and, "the war might have ended within four to six months".27 President Clinton also felt:
the closest we ever were to settling that [politically] was when the Serbs and the Croats thought that the Europeans were going to go along with my proposal to lift the arms embargo and to make standby air power.28

Although the evidence suggests that the overall benefits were in lifting the arms embargo, Britain refused and objected very firmly. Why? Was there a superior motive? The British Defence Secretary, Malcolm Rifkind gave some insight to the thinking of the government when he was asked by Christopher Hutchins regarding the issue. He allegedly replied that lifting the embargo would be the worst of all options because, "it would mean we lost control".29

The US Secretary of State, Warren Christopher, further enlightened us, when he allegedly let slip that Prime Minister John Major had told him that if the arms embargo was lifted by the US, he felt that his government would fall.30

SAFE AREAS
One piece of action the UN took was to designate six towns as "safe areas". On April 16 1993, Security Council Resolution 819 declared Srebrenica a safe area and on May 6 five other towns Sarajevo, Tuzla, Zepa, Gorazde and Bihac were also given the same status.31 However, the concept of safe areas was unclear and brought with it a major problem in the principles of peacekeeping. When Srebrenica was declared the first safe area, the UN were asked regarding the lives of the people inside, General Wehlgren stated that they and Srebrenica were now "protected by the blue flag of the UN." And General Morillon even stated that a further attack would mean, "a declaration of war against the entire world".32 But in July 1995, the city fell completely, 40,000 people fled,33 upto 2,700 men were massacred 34 and as of 22 January 1996, 7,000 men were unaccounted for.35

The principle aim of the safe areas was to protect the Muslims in towns surrounded by Serbian artillery with the aid of demilitarized zones. But the Muslim civilians in this war were not just trapped civilians but as Susan Woodward has pointed out, "they were its intended subject".36 Therefore, by protecting them and threatening the Serbs with air strikes, the UN were compromising their neutrality. At the same time it left the victims more vulnerable, for they were demilitarized with no or very little protection from the UN or NATO. For the mandate still did not allow the UN to return fire if the defenseless civilians were massacred, only if they themselves were under attack.37 In his address to the UN Security Council on the issue Arria said, "we should call them what they are: ghettos, refugee camps, open jails, areas under threat; but we should never be so brazen to call them 'safe areas'".38 The safe areas actually gathered the people together in one place for the slaughter.

In April 1994, an attack started on Gorazde which was holding 60,000 people who were left without food, water or electricity and no convoys were getting through to them. In the words of the Bosnian Deputy Prime Minister, Hadzo Efendic, they were like "sacrificial lambs".39 The protection given to them was such that as the situation became tense, Sir Michael Rose ordered the SAS team out of the city and later the aid workers were also evacuated, and in a letter to Boutros Boutros Ghali Izetbegovic wrote, "the so called safe area has become the most unsafe place in the world".40 Although some UNPROFOR troops were later sent.

In the safe area of Sarajevo, up to 500 shells a day were falling on the city, and the UN troops deployed around the city, in accordance with their mandate would count them, track them, record the dead and report the findings. This was the extent of their mandate.41 When in July 1995, the town fell to the Serbs between 6,000 and 7,000 Muslims are thought to have been massacred.

Throughout this chapter western inaction has been discussed, but Schoenfeld asks whether it was really inaction? For was it inaction or action when James Baker in June 1991 declared that the US would not recognise the independence of Slovenia and Croatia which told Milosevic that his actions would not be opposed, and soon after which the attack on Croatia began. Also, was it action or inaction when upon Yugoslavia's request UN Resolution 713 was passed and the arms embargo was imposed leaving Bosnia defenseless. Schoenfeld also asks whether it was action or inaction when the Muslims were demilitarized in safe areas but the siege and shelling of the city was allowed to continue. The list can go on and on. 42

References for Chapter Three :

1. Michael Dewar, 'Intervention in Bosnia - The Case Against', in The World Today, Vol. 49, No.2, p. 33
2. Ed Vulliamy, Seasons in Hell. Understaning Bosnia's War, London: Simon and Schuster, 1994, p. 123
3. James Gow, in Alex Danchev and Thomas Halverson (eds), International Perspectives on the Yugoslav Conflict, London: Macmillan Press Ltd., 1996, p. 94
4. Laura Silber and Allan Little, The Death of Yugoslavia, London: Penguin Books BBC Books, 1995, p. 319
5. ibid., p. 347
6. ibid.
7. ibid., p. 351
8. ibid., p. 352
9. Warren Zimmermann, 'The Last Ambassodar a Memoir of the Collapse of Yugoslavia', in Foreign Affairs, Vol. 74, No. 2
10. Rabia Ali and Lawrence Lifschultz (eds), Why Bosnia? Writings on the Balkan War, Strong Creek: The Pamphleteer's Press, Inc., 1993, p. xxvii

11. Noel Malcolm, Bosnia A Short History, London: Macmillan, 1994, p. 243

12. Mark Thompson, A Paper House. The Endings of Yugoslavia, London: Vintage, 1992, p. 329

13. Malcolm, op. cit.

14. Gow, op. cit. P. 92

15. Rabia Ali and Lawrence Lifschultz (eds) op. cit., p. xxviii

16. Philip J. Cohen, 'Ending the War and Securing Peace in Former Yugoslavia', In Stjepan G. Mestrovic (ed), Genocide After Emotion. The Postemotional Balkan War, London: Routledge, 1996, p. 36

17. Mujeeb R. Khan, 'Bosnia-Herzegovina and the Crisis of the Post-Cold War International System', in East European Politics and Societies, Vol. 9, No. 3, p. 487

18. Norman Cigar, Genocide in Bosnia. The Policy of "Ethnic Cleansing", College Station: Texas A & M University Press, 1995, p. 167

19. Rabia Ali and Lawrence Lifschultz (eds) op. cit., p. xxviii

20. ibid., p. xxx

21. James J. Sadkovitch, 'The Response of the American Media to Balkan Neo-Nationalisms', in Stjepan G. Mestrovic (ed), Genocide After Emotion. The Postemotional Balkan War, London: Routledge, 1996, p. 132.

22. Cigar, op. cit., p. 170

23. Sabrina Petra Ramet, 'The Bosnian War and the Diplomacy of Accommodation' in Current History, Vol. 93, No. 586, p. 384

24. Mohamed Sacirbey, 'End of the Line. An Open Letter to the British Public' in New Statesman and Society, 28 July 1995

25. International Herald Tribune, 10-11 December 1994, cited in Khan, op. cit., p. 487

26. Stjepan G. Mestrovic (ed), Genocide After Emotion. The Postemotional Balkan War, London: Routledge,1996, pp. 210-211 & p. 34

27. Malcolm, op. cit., p. 244

28. Cigar, op. cit., p. 174

29. Ali & Lifschultz (eds), op. cit., p. xlvii

30. Christopher Bennett, Yugoslavia's Bloody Collapse. Causes, Course and Consequences, London: Hurst & Company, 1995, p. 203

31. Susan L. Woodward, Balkan Tragedy. Chaos and Dissolution After the Cold War, Washington: The Brookings Institution, 1995, pp. 412-413

32. Laura Silber and Allan Little, The Death of Yugoslavia, London: Penguin Books BBC Books, 1995, p. 304

33. ibid.

34. The Guardian, 11 August 1995

35. The Guardian, 22 January 1996

36. Woodward, op. cit., p. 319

37. Malcolm, op. cit., p. 250

38. Ali & Lifschultz (eds), op. cit., p. xxx

39. ibid.

40. Silber and Little, op. cit., pp. 368-369

41. Kate Hoey & Calum Macdonald et al., 'Shot By Both Sides' in New Statesman and Society, 29 October 1993, p. 25

42. G. Schoenfeld, 'Psychoanalytic Dimensions of the West's Involvement in the Third Balkan War' in Mestrovic (ed), op. cit., p. 168

CHAPTER FOUR

SOME MISCONCEPTIONS

Those politicians and army officers against the use of military force and intervention used words to confuse the issue and to swing public opinion in their favour. One such case was calling the conflict 'civil war' as James Hogue editor of Foreign Affairs has claimed,1 or blaming 'ethnic hatreds' as did

Warren Christopher,2 or like Douglas Hogg putting it down to "ethnic and historic", tensions.3 The aim of all of this was to say that because the conflict and hatred goes back centuries intervening would not solve anything, there is nothing anyone can do. The 'civil war' argument boils down to the same thing, that becoming mixed up in a civil war could be very costly and there are no quick or easy solutions. This also meant that there was no justification or legitimacy for intervention. However, such arguments are far from the truth. Ivo Banac Professor of History at Yale University argues that these debates only help to legitimise and implement policies designed "to abandon Bosnia and do nothing".4 Bosnia has existed since the Middle Ages in which Serbs, Croats and Muslims have coexisted. Mark Thompson writes that the notion of ethnic war originated in Belgrade and Banja Luka and argues that the Bosnian, Serb and Croat nations were indistinguishable from each other5 and since 1945 over 25% of marriages have been mixed.6

The war in Banac's view was "essentially a war of aggression conducted by Serbia against an internationally recognised independent state".7 The people of Bosnia were living in harmony until Serbia, Milosevic and their nationalism ignited nationalist sentiments, in an overall aim of creating a Greater Serbia in which all Serbs could live. After Croatia's and Slovenia's independence, by the time Bosnia. Herzegovina voted for independence what remained of the former Yugoslavia was basically a Greater Serbia consisting of Serbia and Montenegro. In 1989 Milosevic and the JNA revoked the autonomous status, of Kosovo and Vojvodina. Thereafter, they launched a war on the Krajina region of Croatia and finally started a war in Bosnia, all in the pursuit of a Greater Serbia. A year prior to Bosnia's declaration of independence, Tudjman of Croatia and Milosevic of Serbia had already agreed upon the carving up of Bosnia; independence was not part of the equation.8 The blame for war and the atrocities that came with it, to a great extent belongs to Milosevic, who with his dreams of a Greater Serbia had taken control and was at the centre of everything . By July 1991, there was evidence that he was arming the Bosnian Serbs and was controlling Karadzic. In May 1992 Milosevic announced that all soldiers in the JNA from Serbia or Montenegro would be withdrawn. In reality, whether any withdrew and if so how many, was not checked,9 but what is for certain is that soldiers from Serbia under the direct control of Milosevic took a central part in the war. Even so, this little exercise gave Western diplomats another excuse to proclaim a civil war.

A paramilitary commander, Branislav Vakic, testified at The Hague Tribunal that he and his men were armed and trained by Milosevic's agents in Belgrade, and that they fought alongside Serbian interior ministry forces in Bosnia in 1993, a year after Milosevic claimed his troops had been withdrawn. Also at the Tribunal a former Belgrade police chief, Marko Nicovic, testified that thousands of prisoners were released from Serbian prisons to join paramilitary units and in return they were promised shortened sentences.10 A former senior member of the Serbian secret police, Cedomir Mihailovic defected with some invaluable documents, including orders from the Serbian State Security Services in Belgrade regarding the running of concentration camps in Bosnia.11 And even as late as at the time of the Dayton Agreement, General Morillon allegedly said he was told by Milosevic that the Serbian army was fighting in Bosnia.12

Thus, it is clear that Milosevic and Belgrade by igniting nationalist sentiments started the war in Bosnia, and throughout the war were engaged in all aspects of it from the training and supplying of men through to the running of concentration camps. The cause of it all was the dream of a Greater Serbia, not ethnic or historical hatred.

According to the UN Kalshoven Commission the conflict was international not internal. Proclaiming the war to be a civil war or internal, benefited Milosevic and the Serbs during the war, but also benefits them after the war. For in internal or civil wars, indicted war criminals cannot be prosecuted for 'grave breaches' or 'war crimes', but only for the crime of genocide and crimes against humanity. For crimes against humanity government planning is necessary; and for genocide, the intent to destroy, even in part a racial, ethnic, national or religious group is a condition. For 'war crimes' or 'grave breaches' these conditions do not apply but these can only be prosecuted in international wars, not internal or civil wars.13

Lord Owen was of the opinion that in the beginning it was a case of aggression but then turned into a civil war with fighting in between villages. However, this can only occur if events are haphazard, out of control and occurring at the local level without a grand strategy, or control from a higher authority, and this was not so in Bosnia.14

Further to this, since April 1992, Bosnia has been an independent state, and although Karadzic called all Serbs to boycott the referendum, many did not and 66% of the total population turned out and voted in favour of independence, which was recognised by the EC and US.15

Another such ploy has been to water down the atrocities committed by the Serbs, by saying that all sides are equal and that all sides have committed atrocities. As Warren Christopher stated, "there are atrocities on all sides".16 And Major General Mackenzie used an analogy of three serial killers, where one kills fifteen people, another kills ten and the last kills five. He argues that we will not say the last one is good but they are all bad.17 Denis Skinner took it a step further and is alleged to have said, "There is ethnic cleansing right here of miners in the pits, so don't tell me about ethnic cleansing", implying that no atrocities were taking place.18

It must also be remembered that during World War two the allies committed various war crimes, for example the bombing of Dresden, fire bombing various cities and not forgetting Nagasaki or Hiroshima. But no reasonable politician, journalist, academic or observer has concluded that the allies and the Nazis are equally to blame or are like 'serial killers' with a different tally of murders to their names; the two just cannot be compared.19

Another such distortion was the claim made by various prominent people that to gain public attention and to draw in the world powers the Muslims were killing their own people. Such notions were whispered and spread at the right places, which had the effect of making the victims into the criminals and victimisers. On Saturday 5 February, a mortar bomb dropped on the Sarajevo market killing, 69 people and injuring 200. Karadzic denied responsibility and later blamed the Muslims for planting the bomb, which was later also repeated by politicians and UN personnel. Later an UNPROFOR crater analysis proved nothing, for the missile was diverted by an overhead canopy. The UN did determine the direction from where the missile was fired, but both sides had positions there. General Rose endeavoured relentlessly for two weeks to put off the threatening air strikes, and if the slightest bit of evidence would have been found, that the Muslims had fired at their own people, he would have used it to block the air strikes, but no evidence was found. Although commonsense says the mortar had been fired by those people who had shelled the city for months and had killed thousands of other civilians.20 When in May 1992 a bomb killed 22 people waiting in a bread queue in Sarajevo, General Mackenzie allegedly aired the view that the Muslims were killing their own people, although no evidence was produced, 21 but other UN officials did refute this argument.22

References for Chapter Four

1. Rabia Ali and Lawrence Lifschultz (eds), Why Bosnia? Writings on the Balkan War, Strong Creek: The Pamphleteer's Press, Inc., 1993, p. xix
2. Laura Silber and Allan Little, The Death of Yugoslavia, London: Penguin Books BBC Books, 1995, p. 319
3. James Gow, in Alex Danchev and Thomas Halverson (eds), International Perspectives on the Yugoslav Conflict, London: Macmillan Press Ltd., 1996, p. 89
4. Ali & Lifschultz (eds), op. cit., p. xx
5. Mark Thompson, A Paper House. 'The Final Solution of Bosnia-Herzegovina', in Ali & Lifschultz (eds) op. cit., p. 174
6. Ed Vulliamy, Seasons in Hell. Understanding Bosnia's War. London: Simon & Schuster, 1994 p. 39
7. Ali & Lifschultz (eds), op. cit., p. xx
8. ibid., p. xxv
9. Noel Malcolm, Bosnia A Short History, London: Macmillan, 1994, p. 238
10. The Guardian, 3 February 1997
11. The Guardian, 14 April 1995
12. The Guardian, 12 January 1996

13. Theodor Meron, 'The Case for War Crimes Trials in Yugoslavia' in Foreign Affairs, Vol. 72, No. 3, pp. 128-132

14. Norman Cigar, Genocide in Bosnia. The Policy of "Ethnic Cleansing", College Station: Texas A & M University Press, 1995, p. 121

15. Christopher Bennett, Yugoslavia's Bloody Collapse. Causes, Course and Consequences, London: Hurst & Company, 1995, p. 168

16. Silber & Little, op. cit., p. 320

17. Cigar, op. Cit.

18. The Guardian, 15 July 1995

19. Stjepan G. Mestrovic (ed), Genocide After Emotion. The Postemotional Balkan War, London: Routledge, 1996, pp. 7-8

20. Silber & Little, op. cit., p. 344

21. ibid.

22. Mujeeb R. Khan, 'Bosnia-Herzegovina and the Crisis of the Post-Cold War International System', in East European Politics and Societies, Vol. 9, No. 3, p. 491

CHAPTER FIVE

REWARDING THE AGGRESSOR

Great parallels can be made between Milosevic and the Bosnian tragedy on the one hand, and Hitler and the Holocaust on the other. As Hitler claimed that the German minorities in Poland and Czechoslovakia were been persecuted, Milosevic alleged that the Serbs were also victims and oppressed. Both used this to gain support and as an excuse for intervention and annexation of land[1]. Both used the sentiment of nationalism, were ruthless in their pursuit of power and gave Europe a genocide each within half a century, albeit on a different scale.

The reaction of the international organisations and the western powers to both have also been identical. Like the Serbian aggression the early Nazi aggression was condoned and justified by the western powers. Professor Ivo Banac of Yale University saw Karadzic as Konrad Henlein and the Serbian Democratic Party as the Sudetendeutsche Partei.[2] Drawing similarities with Czechoslovakia and its President, Eduard Benes, who was forced into exile to London, Izetbegovic told John Burns of the New York Times, "instead of Munich, it is Geneva. Instead of little Czechoslovakia it is little Bosnia. Instead of negotiating for real peace, they are negotiating for an imaginary one. And instead of Benes, it is me".[3]

However where they both differed was that after a while the western powers regarded Hitler as a threat to their interests, which provoked a stern military reaction, but Serbia and Milosevic did not pose this threat, and did not warrant intervention.[4] And as Dzemal Sokolovic has pointed out:

World War II began with a declaration of war and ended with genocide as a byproduct, but this genocide in Bosnia was the immediate aim, and the war was the consequence of the crime, not the cause.[5]

In Bosnia all the major peace plans drawn up by the international community recognised Serbian aggression and territorial conquests, including the final one. The Muslims argued that this would not only reward the Serbs but would at the same time leave them all the more vulnerable.[6]

The Dayton Peace Agreement which ended the war gave the Muslim-Croat federation 51% of the territory and the Serbs 49%. Thus, even this was accepting Serbian aggression and rewarding ethnic cleansing. However, Various diplomats have argued that Serb aggression has not been rewarded, but even before the war they owned majority of the land, although the Muslim population was larger. As did Lord Owen, who claimed that the Serbs owned 60% of the land before the war. But this is not true, for the Serbs owned a lot of private land because Muslims were dispossessed during the inter-war years. And even if we accept that it belonged to the Serbs, the total private land of Bosnia is 2.375 million hectares, and the total area of Bosnia is 5.113 million hectares. Which means the total private land is equal to 46% of the total area of Bosnia. And if the Serbs owned 60% of the private land it still only equals 28% of Bosnia, not 60%. Thus, we can clearly say that the Dayton Peace Agreement has rewarded aggression and accepted ethnic cleansing. Also, as feared by the Muslims of Bosnia, the settlement did leave them more vulnerable, for Bosnia was divided along ethnic lines.7

For peace in Bosnia and for future peace in the world it is necessary that the indicted war criminals are brought to trial, but no genuine efforts are being made towards this. The international community even after the war are walking the same line as during the war, and claim that by arresting the war criminals especially the leaders, peace and stability in the region will not remain. Similarly, the UN forces even after the peace agreement have problems with their mandate. This time in regards to the arresting of war criminals.

The War Crimes Tribunal which was established to bring the war criminals of the Bosnian tragedy to justice has also been undermined in many ways. It has difficulties bringing the accused to custody and gaining evidence that can stand up to cross examination.8 The UN Kalshoven Commission which is responsible for providing evidence of war crimes only consists of two lawyers with no investigators of its own. In comparison, the Nuremburg prosecutors had hundreds of lawyers and investigators.9

In October 1995, the US government was accused by the tribunal of not handing over information regarding the attacks on Srebrenica. Germany and France are also alleged to be withholding information.10

Although UN Security Council Resolution 827 states that all countries must cooperate and the UN Genocide Convention states that the guilty have to be pursued and punished, in August 1996, IFOR troops were searching a building for illegal weapons not realising that the war criminal Ratko Mladic was inside. Upon realising they left without arresting him.11 On December 10 1996, the International Police Force met the war criminal Radovan Karadzic in Pale, but did not arrest him. As of March 1997, the International Criminal Tribunal had indicted 74 suspects and 67 were still at large.12

The Dayton Peace Agreement states:
no person who is serving a sentence imposed by the International Tribunal for the former Yugoslavia, and no person who is under indictment by the Tribunal and who has failed to comply with an order to appear before the tribunal, may stand as a candidate or hold any appointive, elective, or other public office in the territory of Bosnia and Herzegovina.13

However, in Bosnia-Herzegovina not only did indicted war criminals stand for elections but the Organisation for Security and Co-operation in Europe (OSCE) gave £150,000 for the election campaign of the indicted war criminal Zelko Raznjatovic, better known as Arkan, who is even wanted by Interpol and seven European countries for activities before the war.14

Selma Hecimovic, a schoolteacher in Bosnia says, "it is the end of civilisation if somebody can do all these things and then be rewarded at the end".15

References for Chapter Five

1. Christopher Bennett, Yugoslavia's Bloody Collapse. Causes, Course and Consequences, London: Hurst & Company, 1995, p. 243
2. Rabia Ali and Lawrence Lifchultz (eds), Why Bosnia? Writings on the Balkan War, Strong Creek: The Pamphleteer's Press, Inc., 1993, p. xx
3. ibid., p. xxi
4. Bennett, op. cit., p. 244
5. Stjepan G. Mestrovic (ed), Genocide After Emotion. The Postemotional Balkan War, London: Routledge, 1996, p. 2
6. Norman Cigar, Genocide in Bosnia. The Policy of "Ethnic Cleansing", College Station: Texas A & M University Press, 1995, p. 150
7. ibid., p. 119
8. Bennett, op. cit., p. 239

9. Theodor Meron, 'The Case for War Crimes Trials in Yugoslavia' in Foreign Affairs, Vol. 72, No. 3, p. 125

10. The Guardian, 28 November 1995

11. The Guardian, 8 may 1997

12. The Guardian, 26 March 1997

13. The Guardian, 13 September 1996

14. The Guardian, 5 September 1996

15. Ed Vulliamy, Seasons in Hell. Understanding Bosnia's War. London: Simon & Schuster, 1994 p. 201

CONCLUSION

It is clear that the so called war in Bosnia was no war as such, but was a one sided aggression against a defenseless people. The aggression brought with it ethnic cleansing of the Muslims and genocide. This was not a consequence of war but was a goal in itself, planned and implemented systematically in pursuit of a Greater Serbia.

The international community, for various reasons, were unwilling to recognise Serbia as the aggressors, and to treat them likewise. The result was that the aggressor and the aggressed, the victimiser and the victim, the persecutor and the persecuted, the attacker and the besieged all were treated equally. In so doing, the fact that Bosnia-Herzegovina was a recognised independent state, and a member of the UN was forgotten.

Throughout the conflict the western leaders were concerned of a spill-over, and a wider Balkan conflict. But, what their actions did not take into account was that no other state besides Serbia was looking to create a greater nation. Without doubt there is discontent among other peoples like the Albanians in Kosovo, but this again is due to persecution by the Serbian government. Therefore, the starting point for peace in the Balkans has to be the containment of Serbia and this has to be militarily as the Bosnian tragedy has shown Milosovic and Serbia only understand the language of force. The very recent (February 1998) unrest and persecutions in Kosovo instigated by Milosevic has verified this.

The implications of the tragedy in Bosnia-Herzegovina are far greater than originally seems. The international community did not become involved militarily because generally no vital interests were at stake. If they were willing the tragedy could have been stopped before it begun. This implies that morality has no part to play in the 'New World Order'. Also, by imposing and retaining the arms embargo the international community practically aided the aggressor and made the victim defenseless. Further to this, the Helsinki Accords and Geneva Conventions were also violated and undefended by the international community, which could mean that they no longer hold any value and are no longer the universally accepted code of practice. In addition to this, acceptance of aggression by the international community is a signal for not only Milosevic but all tyrants that force and aggression pays.

The conflict also made apparent that the European Community has a long way to go before it can proclaim that its member states act as one cohesively, in issues of defense and security. It has also shown that even after the collapse of communism, Russia is still a major force and player in international politics. The crisis has also undermined the future of NATO which was unable to act decisively, independent of the UN. The credibility of the UN was also greatly reduced by the crisis, and the importance of differentiating between peacekeeping and peace enforcement was clearly highlighted.

Finally, there is no doubt that the international community could have stopped or reduced the extent of the tragedy, if they so desired. But should they have? If moral principles and humanity is still to be upheld in the world, then yes.

Bibliography

Bibliography of Books:

Ali , Rabia and Lifschultz, Lawrence (eds), Why Bosnia? Writings on the Balkan War, Stony Creek: The pamphleteer's Press Inc., 1993

Bell-Fialkoff, Andrew Ethnic Cleansing, London: Macmillan, 1996

Bennett, Christopher Yugoslavia's Bloody Collapse. Causes, Course and Consequences, London: Hurst & Company, 1995

Carter, F. W. and Norris, H. T. The Changing Shape of the Balkans, London: UCL Press, 1996

Cigar, Norman Genocide in Bosnia. The Policy of Ethnic Cleansing, College Station: Texas A & M University Press, 1995

Crnobrnja, Mihailo The Yugoslav Drama, London: I.B. Tauris Publishers, 1994

Danchev, Alex and Halverson, Thomas (eds), International Perspectives on the Yugoslav Conflict, London: Macmillan Press Ltd., 1996

Fawcett, J.E.S. The Application of the European Convention on Human Rights, Oxford: Clarendon press, 1969

Glenny, Misha The fall of Yugoslavia, The Third Balkan War, London: Penguin Books, 1993

Gutman, Roy A witness to Genocide, Shaftesbury: Element, 1993

Judah, Tim The Serbs, History, Myth and the Destruction of Yugoslavia, London: Yale University Press, 1997

Mestrovic, Stjepan G. (ed), Genocide After Emotion. The Postemotional Balkan War, London: Routledge, 1996

Pavkovic, Aleksandar The Fragmentation of Yugoslavia. Nationalism in a Multinational state, London: Macmillan Press Ltd., 1997

Rieff, David Slaughterhouse. Bosnia and the Failure of the West, London: Vintage, 1995

Silber, Laura and Little, Allan The Death of Yugoslavia, London: Penguin Books BBC Books, 1995

Thompson, Mark A Paper House. The Endings of Yugoslavia, London: Vintage, 1992

Vulliamy, Ed Seasons in Hell. Understanding Bosnia's War, London: Simon and Schnster, 1994

Woodward, Susan L. Balkan Tragedy. Chaos and Dissolution After the Cold War, Washington: The Brookings Institution, 1995

The United Nations and Human Rights 1945-1995, The United Nations Blue Book Series, Vol. 7, 1995

Bibliography of Articles

Atta, Dale Van 'The Folly of UN Peacekeeping', in Reader's Digest, October 1995, pp.118- 123

Betts, Richard K. 'The Delusion of Impartial Intervention', in Foreign Affairs, Vol. 73, no. 6, pp. 20-33

Brenner, Michael J. 'EC: Confidence Lost', in Foreign Policy, No. 91, Summer 1993, pp. 24-4

Burg, Steven L 'Why Yugoslavia Fell Apart' in Current History, Vol. 92, No. 577, pp.357- 363

Calic, Marie-Janine The Serbian Question in International Politics', in Aussenpolitik, Vol. 45, No. 2, pp. 146-155

Cohen, Lenard J. 'Bosnia and Herzegovina: Fragile Peace in a Segmented State' in Current History, Vol. 95, No. 599, pp.103-112

Dewar, Michael 'Intervention in Bosnia - The Case Against', in The World Today, Vol. 49, No.2, p. 32-34

Featherston, A. B. et al 'UNPROFOR: Some Observations from a Conflict Resolution Perspective', in International Peacekeeping, Vol. 1, No. 2, pp. 179-203

Freedman, Lawrence 'Why the West Failed' in Foreign Policy, No. 97, Winter 1994-95, pp. 53-69

Gompert, David 'How to Defeat Serbia' in Foreign Affairs, Vol. 73, No. 4, pp. 30-47

Gow, James and Dandeker, Christopher 'Peace-support Operations: The Problem of Legitimation', in The World Today, Vol. 51, No. 8-9, pp. 171-174

Gow, James 'Towards a Settlement in Bosnia: The Military Dimension ', in The World Today, Vol. 50, No.5, pp. 96- 99

Hibbert, Reginald 'The War in Bosnia: Can the Balkans be saved from Balkanisation?' In The World Today Vol. 51, No. 8-9, pp. 155-157

Hoey Kate & Macdonald, Calum et al., 'Shot By Both Sides' in New Statesman and Society, 29 October 1993, p. 25

Khan, Mujeeb R. 'Bosnia-Herzegovina and the Crisis of the Post-Cold War International System', in East European Politics and Societies, Vol. 9, No. 3, pp. 459-498

Koslowski, Gerd 'Bosnia: Failure of the Institutions and of the Balance of Power in Europe, in Aussenpolitik, Vol. 47, No. 4 , pp. 359-367

Macdonald, Calum 'Rose-tinted Spectacles', in New Statesman and Society, 10 February 1995, p. 23

Mazowiecki. Tadeusz 'Will to Disaster', in Index on censorship, Vol., 24, No. 5, pp. 67-72

Meron, Theodor 'The Case for War Crimes Trials in Yugoslavia', in Foreign Affairs, Vol. 72, No. 3, pp. 122-135

Ramet, Sabrina Petra 'The Bosnian War and the Diplomacy of Accommodation' in Current History, Vol. 93, No. 586, p. 380-385

Ramet, Sabrina Petra 'The Yugoslav Crisis and the West: Avoiding "Vietnam" and Blundering into "Abyssinia", in East European Politics and Societies, Vol. 8 No. 1, pp. 189-219

Ruggie, John Gerard 'Wandering in the Void. Charting the UN's New Strategic Role, in Foreign Affairs, Vol. 72, No. 5, pp. 26-31

Sacirbey, Mohamed 'End of the Line. An Open Letter to the British Public' in New Statesman and Society, 28 July 1995, pp.14-15

Sadkovich, James J. 'War, Genocide and the Need to Lift the Embargo on Bosnia and Croatia', in Journal of Croatian Studies, Vol. 32, No. 33, pp. 132-133

Sherr, James 'Doomed To Remain a Great Power' in The World Today Vol. 52, No.1, pp. 8-12

Sloan, Stanley R. 'US Perspectives on NATO's Future', in International Affairs, Vol. 71, No.2, pp. 217-231

Williams, Michael 'The Best Chance for Peace in Bosnia' in The World Today, Vol. 52, No. 1, pp. 4-7

Zimmermann, Warren 'The Last Ambassodar a Memoir of the Collapse of Yugoslavia', in Foreign Affairs, Vol. 74, No. 2

Bibliography of Newspapers

The Daily Jang (London)

The Guardian

The Observer

END

www.ingramcontent.com/pod-product-compliance
Lightning Source LLC
Chambersburg PA
CBHW051953280526
45789CB00009B/3270